Stained Glass Windows *from a* Different Perspective

Title: "We Survived The Vortex"

Wardell
PUBLICATIONS INC

Cataloging in Publication Data

Levy, Mark
  Windows from a Different Perspective: Collection Five
ISBN 0-919985-34-3

1. Levy, Mark
2. Glass painting and staining - United States.
3. Glass craft - Patterns - Catalogs.   I. Title

NK5398.L48A4 2001   748.59   C2001-900759-0

Windows from a Different Perspective, Collection Five is Copyright © 2002 by Wardell Publications Inc.

Printed and bound in Thailand by Phongwarin Printing Ltd.

Published simultaneously in Canada and USA by Wardell Publications Inc

Distributed worldwide, inquire for authorized dealer list

EMail at: info@wardellpublications.com

Web site at: www.wardellpublications.com

Windows from a Different Perspective

Studio Designer Series Collection Five

Studio Designer and Book Author
Mark Levy

Art Glass Fabrication
Mark Levy • Tami Stephens

Photography
Mark Levy • David Solzberg • Martin Fine
Tom Bernard • John Zimmerman

Publisher
Randy Wardell

Book Layout & Typography
Carole Wardell • Randy Wardell

Special Thanks from the Author

Lee and Mike Levy for their love and support; Tami Stephens for her wonderful creative input and incredible talent in bringing my works to life; Bill Punches for his time and inventive creations; Ben Halpern for introducing me to glass; Ron Mazza for letting me watch a master; the many architects and designers who've trusted my abilities; to my clients for placing their faith in me; and a VERY SPECIAL thank you to Linda J. Singer for her wisdom, patience and insight, without whom none of what I have or do would be possible.

Published by

To receive our electronic newsletter or to send suggestions please contact us
by E-mail at: info@wardellpublications.com or visit our web site at: www.wardellpublications.com

Title: "Looking Beyond The Obvious
– 2nd Exposure"

Foreword

The glass creations of Mark Levy have graced public, private, and corporate collections for over 24 years. His works have been described as bold, complex, and architectural, with an uncompromising attention to detail.

Mark is keenly aware that his cutting edge designs will have an effect on the viewer and meticulously composes each project with careful glass selection. He has a unique combination of intrinsic artistic ability and extensive architectural training which enables him to effectively create an artistic reality that is in harmony with the surrounding space. Mark's personal conviction is to exceed the expectations of his clients by challenging and expanding his artistic boundaries.

"My designs are a personal interpretation of the surprising events that have shaped and guided my life. Like most people, I often wonder about the significance of these uncontrollable situations. The choices that I have made at these times have defined me as a person and helped me to develop my unique viewpoint. It is these moments of challenge and choice that have offered clarity. They have pushed me to evolve personally and artistically.

As an artist, I believe my task is to translate these important experiences into an abstract form. I use the color, light and texture of glass to express myself and to offer the viewer the opportunity to encounter my work, to interpret it for themselves, and to experience a different perspective".

Mark Levy Studio
P.O. Box 4722,
Chatsworth, CA. 91311 USA
Ph: 818-595-1195
E-mail: mlstudio@earthlink.net
Website: www.marklevystudio.com

Section Contents & Style Locator

This locator is loosely structured on the style as indicated by the section title.
Some window designs fit into two or more of these section definitions
Please use this contents page as a sampler guide only.

Section One - Abstract Circles

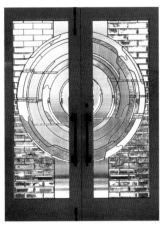

Page 6 to Page 29

Section Two - Tumbling Block Series

Page 30 to Page 41

Section Three - Linear Organics

Page 42 to Page 67

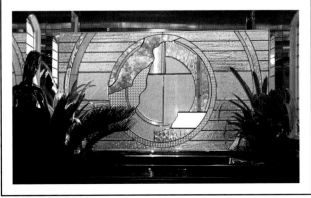

Section Four - Designers Divergence

Page 68 to Page 78

The Day The Appliances Danced

I loved working in my old studio. It was by the railroad tracks in an industrial area and had wonderful natural light. Although it met my requirements, what I was really longing for was an area to have a gallery/showroom, where clients could see autonomous panels, glass sculptures, and new personal works. I looked at over 20 spaces before I found an industrial unit in Chatsworth, CA that was three times the size of my former studio, with the perfect layout for a gallery, a work area, and a kitchen! After I signed a 5 year lease I met with my contractor to plan out the new lighting, walls, and plumbing, and we were set to move in December 15, 1993.

Title (above): "Composition I"
One of the sculptures in the showroom

I discovered that moving 20 years worth of glass was no easy task. The inventory was very extensive but I knew the new storage systems would handle it and more. The remodeling and modifications were completed and we moved in with enough time to have my new years eve party in the new studio. Everything was just the way I had always envisioned my perfect studio would be...a kitchen, office, work area, and most especially, a gallery. For this area, my contractor and I had designed a custom halogen lighting system that hung from the ceiling and allowed for infinite adjustments in height, width and angle. My new pieces, as well as some of my older sculptures, screens, room dividers and autonomous panels, were finally at home in their new gallery setting.

The first month in my new space was wonderful, and all of my clients commented on how well the studio was laid out and appointed. It was a dream come true, a new studio where I could work and have clients over in the perfect setting. I had no way of knowing the ominous change that was close at hand.

Title: "R.I.P. - The Day The Appliances Danced (Funeral For Some Friends)"
Photo at left "Composition I" is the same project prior to the earthquake transformation

Early on the morning of February 17, 1994, the Los Angeles area suffered one of its worst earthquakes ever. The magnitude was 10 times greater than the last one, and the damage far more widespread. The epicenter was in Northridge, the town next to where my new studio was. The images of destruction on

This photograph is an example of the devastation I found upon entering my studio that day.

television left me with a foreboding anxiety for what awaited at my new studio. It took me two full days to gather up the courage to go and check. The complex sustained substantial damage, and my space was not spared. The front door had been jammed shut by the shifting walls so I went in through the shipping door, and my worst fears were confirmed...everything was in shambles. All of the new glass racks, holding 20 years worth of collected inventory were destroyed. The completed panels that had been on my racks waiting for installation were shattered. As I turned the corner, the bottom of my stomach dropped. Everything in the gallery was destroyed, including my new pieces that were scheduled to be in an upcoming juried show. I felt like I had walked into a glass graveyard.

It took me a while to recover from the shock, but then I knew that there had to be something I could do. Every artist, no matter what medium they work in, takes the experiences and images in their life, and composes with them. As I surveyed the destruction all around me, I felt I had to do something constructive, and create something positive out of what had occurred. The old saying, "When Life Gives You Lemons, Make Lemonade" set my course. I took the remains of each piece and created coffins for these

graveyard inhabitants. These were made of Plexiglas, and had "headstones" for each of them. Each coffin was custom fit according to the shape of its remains. I took these "coffins" to the show, and arranged a display that was

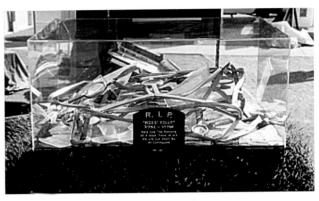

Title: "R.I.P. - Ross's Folly
(Funeral For Some Friends)"

laid out like a graveyard. Each piece was placed on a sod of grass with flowers before it in remembrance. I was amazed and gratified by the respectful attention that these pieces received. It pulled at the hearts of many attendees who seemed to feel a sense of homage. Then when these broken works won 2nd place of show it truly was a cathartic experience. The "Lemonade" I made was bittersweet, but it proved to me that you can create art out of anything in your life...even destruction.

Title: "R.I.P. - Boy's Shouldn't Cry
(Funeral For Some Friends)"

Abstract Circles

Title: "Did U Pay Attention?"

In my opinion the circle is one of the most pleasing and restful forms that occurs in nature. The circle is found everywhere around us and is firmly rooted in our psyche. The planets themselves offer us this visual statement. The circular form intrigues me creatively because it offers boundless design opportunities to explore space and line. It is not finite in the way other shapes are, such as the square or triangle. A pure, elemental circle can have a calm, soothing visual appeal, where a rectangle might not. Yet once modified by contrasting elements, a circle can instead become a source of dramatic complex imagery.

Title: "Strategic Positioning Makes The Difference"

I have found that placing a circle within any architectural opening visually expands that space, no matter the size. The inclusion of a circle within another shape or form lets the eye imagine that the circle continues beyond what is seen. The imagination is stimulated when the mind is free to perceive more than just what it sees before it.

There is something limitless to me about the perception of what a circle is, and what it imparts. As a pebble dropped into water creates radiating circles, I seek to convey that experience in leaded glass. The projects that follow in this section use the circle as a basis to create a sense of calm, as well as drama, for the specific locations they occupy, and for my client's enjoyment.

Title: "The Death Of #5"

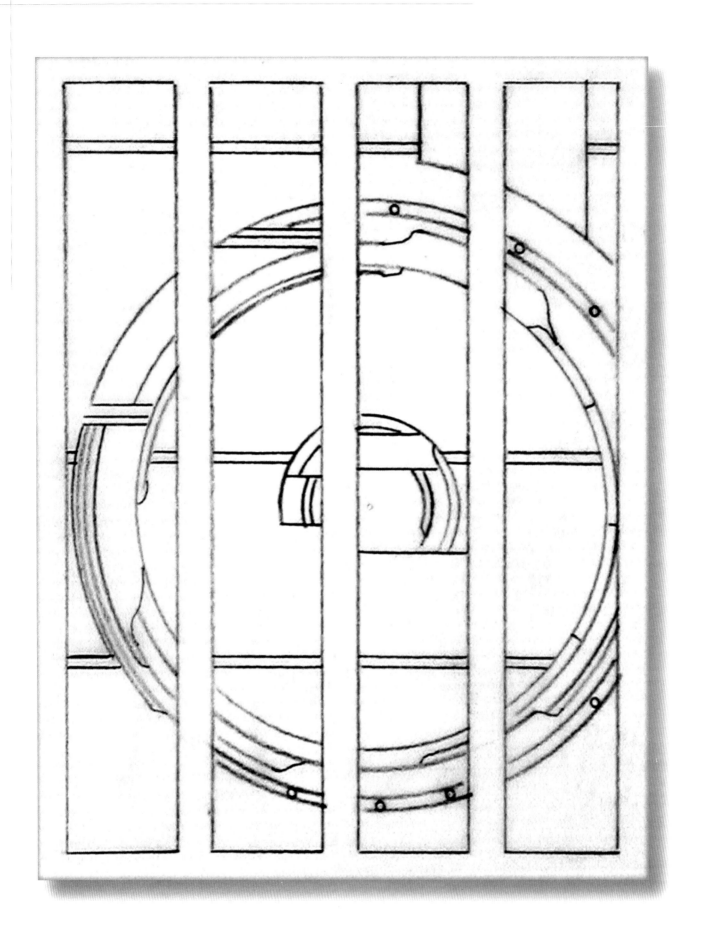

Title: "Circular Turbulence"

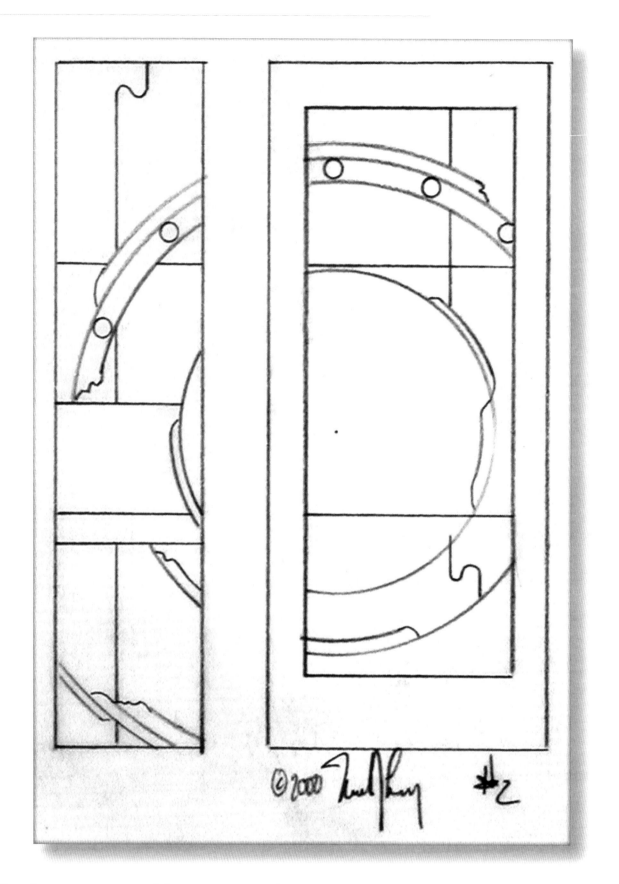

This drawing was one of three concepts I designed for my client's front door and sidelight. After reviewing my presentation, the client selected one with a more pronounced circular motif that she felt pulled the two spaces together and made them appear as one.

This client gave me total creative license on this project to do what I felt best suited the architecture of their new home. It was the first time I had been given complete discretion, and I wanted to reward their confidence with my finest effort. The blueprints indicated the entryway was quite narrow in relation to the rest of the house. I resolved to use a circle as the main feature to visually expand the space within this configuration of doors, sidelights, and transom. I placed the center of the circle above eye level to render more visual height and used the play between negative and positive space to increase the perception of expanse.

Title: "You Ought To Be In Pictures" - Exterior view

Title: "You Ought To Be In Pictures" - Interior view

As a final design decision I used 3/4" thick clear glass and beveled it on both sides to eliminate the distraction of a front and back side to the windows.

The windows are fabricated with 12 different textures of clear glass plus the bevels to create a distinctive and elegant entryway.

Title: "40 Years Of Wandering"

Temple Aliyah in Los Angeles commissioned the installations pictured on these two pages. I worked closely with a design committee that was appointed by the congregation and they requested a contemporary design that utilized a very limited color palette.

Title: "Untitled"

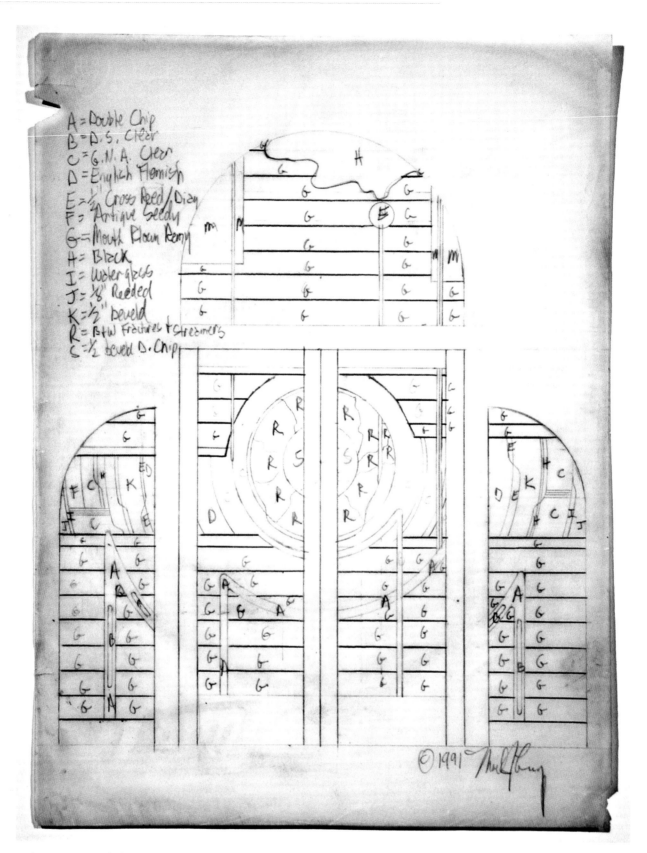

The following legend appears on the drawing:

A = Double Chip
B = D.S. Clear
C = G.N.A. Clear
D = English Flemish
E = 1/4 Cross Reed/Diag
F = Antique Seedy
G = Mouth Blown Remy
H = Black
I = Water glass
J = 1/8" Reeded
K = 1/2" Bevel'd
R = B+W Fractures + Streamers
S = 1/2 Bevel'd D. Chip

© 1991

This proposal drawing was created from dimensions I pulled from the blueprint. However as you can see in the photo on page 17 the actual scale and shape of the sidelights ended up quite different. Changes and alterations are common in custom construction projects which is why I always stipulate in my contract that "on-site" template sizes will determine the final cost.

Title: "Less Is Definitely Enough For Her"

Title: "An Unexpected Expectation" - Detail view

The work of Ed Carpenter had a very strong impact on my early designs. The architectural use of the circular form seemed to be the perfect element to explore line value and symmetry. His sensitivity regarding glass selection was always inspired. This project owes its roots to his groundbreaking contribution to contemporary glasswork.

This home was designed by the well-known modernist architect Richard Neutra. The front door and windows were from the 1940's, and my client requested an organic mural that respected the original integrity of Neutra's design. I developed a new entryway and transom system, 31' (9.6 m) in length and carried the design across this entire expanse. The title "An Unexpected Expectation" refers to my acute awareness that not only was I updating the work of a

Title: "An Unexpected Expectation" - Full view

world renowned architect, but also paying homage to a consummate glass designer whose work had profoundly influenced me. The ownership of the home has changed hands twice since the installation and each subsequent owner has contacted me to learn more about the design.

Title: "The Error Of Eros Arrows"

This client's home is very traditional as you can see by her wallpaper, and the glass colors are in keeping with that soft palette. As we discussed the design possibilities my client favored the notion to use the circles to accentuate the bay window and the arch shape.

Title: "Distant Origins" – Within Room Setting

This client wanted something very modern and bold in her kitchen ceiling to contrast with the moderate neutralism that is prevalent in the rest of the room's design.

Title: "The Complex Nature"

Title: "Breaking The Silence"

These three projects were produced around the same time period, yet each explores very differently how I was using the circle motif to create a sense of drama or calm. It is the unlimited "alterability" of the circle that continues to intrigue me.

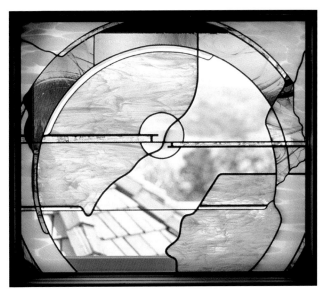

Title: "Off On Another One Of His Tangents"

By comparing this drawing to the finished window on the next page you will see that I elected to raise the last circular band to the top edge of the transom, effectively increasing the perception of height. It is customary to slightly modify a design during fabrication to add visual interest. The beveled "brick" background matches the brick exterior of the home.

Title: "Glass Bricks, Not Blocks"

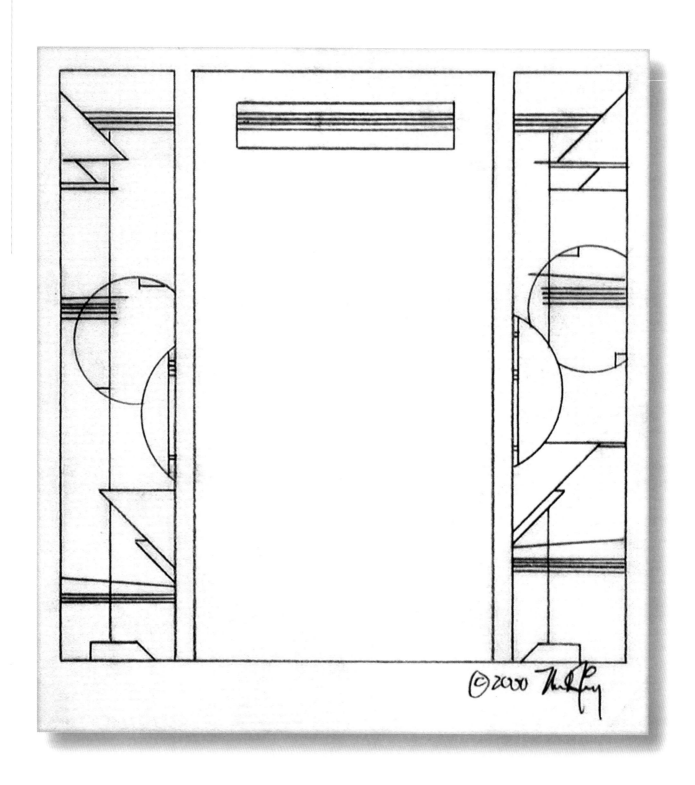

©2000 [signature]

My client selected this proposal from 3 that I presented. The sidelight designs are "symmetrically asymmetrical", and the door insert ties them together. These clients collect the work of the artist Kandinsky, and they asked me to "inject" his aesthetic style into my glass design. The photograph on the bottom of the next page (25) shows the completed installation.

Title: "Composition I"

Title: "Very Special K "

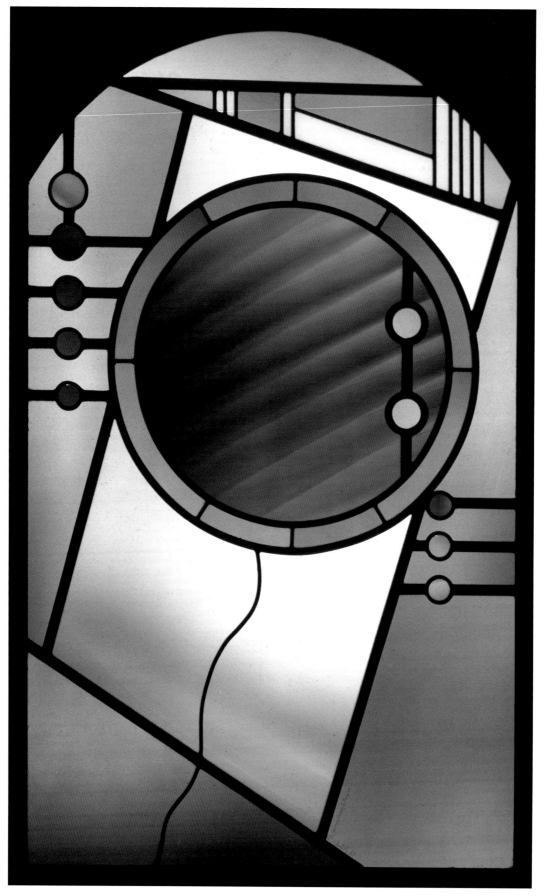

Title: "To Heiress Human, To........"

The sculptural piece titled "All These Extra Pounds Make Me Feel Out Of Bounds" (this page, at bottom right), was one of my first experimental pieces working with the idea of glass shapes moving beyond the bounds of a fixed geometrical perimeter. This sculpture is constructed of leaded glass, mounted in a concrete base. The detail photo (at bottom left) reveals the added touch of painted lead came. I used multi-textured enamel to expand the visual interest. There were a total of five sculptures in this "beyond the bounds" series.

Title: "Simply Irresistible"

Below, a detail photo showing the use of paint to enhance the lead came surface.

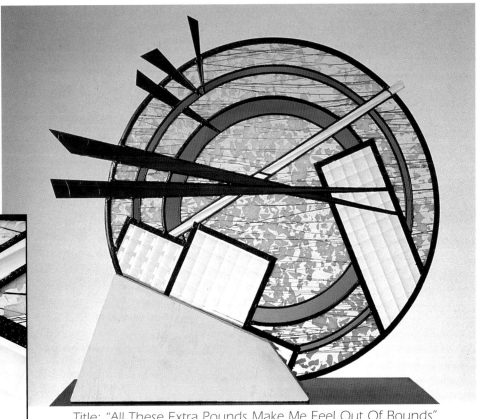

Title: "All These Extra Pounds Make Me Feel Out Of Bounds"

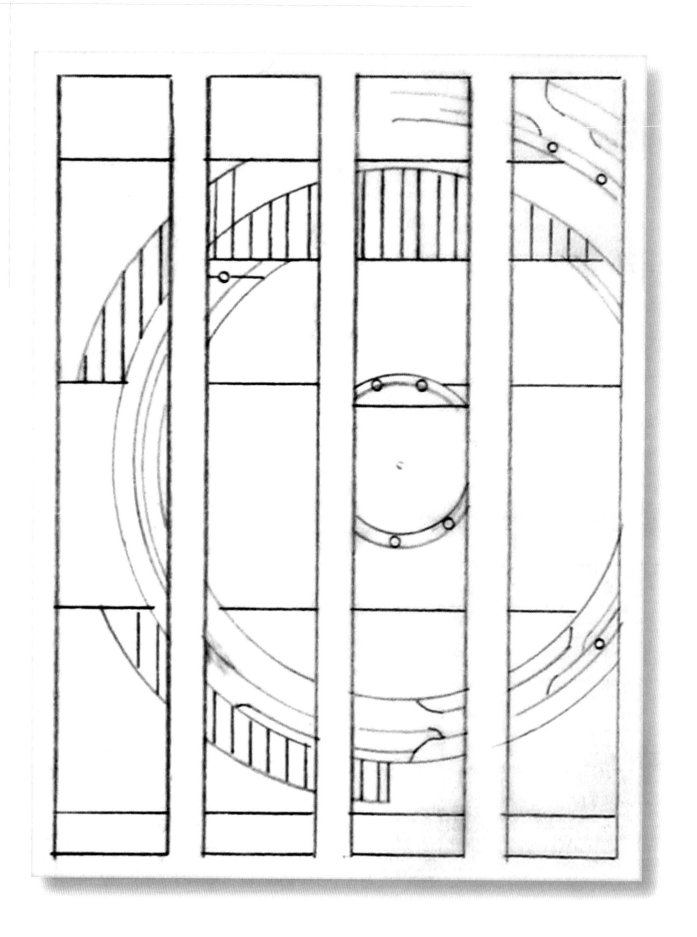

Title: "Opus XVII"

Tumbling Blocks

Title: "I'll Trade You For A Tumble"

Prior to this "Tumbling Block" series my primary focus was on using pure design elements. The emphasis was on the line value of each design and I used predominantly textured clear glass and bevels, rather than color, to avert any distraction from the graphic elements. Then I began to explore how squares and rectangles, found in some of my earlier pieces, might be altered by a sense of movement. The windows shown on page 67 were my earliest investigations in letting squares and rectangles move freely, but were not altered in their shape by that movement. I found myself shifting from a focus on pure graphic design when I yielded to the creative exhilaration of the glass and allowed the energy of color to influence my work. By selecting each piece of glass for its own intrinsic beauty and specific attributes, I was letting my designs become just as much glass driven as design driven. I was working with colors and shapes that I had previously restrained and my designs took on a whole new way of moving and interacting.

Title: "I'll Trade You For A Tumble" - Detail

Title: " The First Tumble" - interior view

There is a wonderful perpetual process as designs take shape. Often as I'm finishing one piece, my mind moves on to visualize the creative direction that my next work might take. An important part of this creative process is to allow your mind to be open to possibilities that may arise that you did not expect. Exploring that direction and where it might lead is a key factor to letting the work evolve. The course that this series has taken has been unexpected in many ways, yet as always I'm guided by my desire to continue growing as an artist.

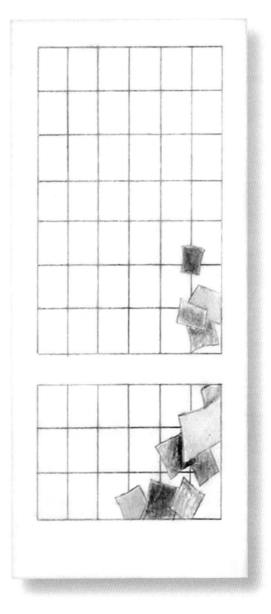

Movement and interaction of these shapes has become my guiding force in this series, and the more works I do the more I find myself designing with a new found freedom. The action and interplay of one component against the next, and how that occurrence changes each piece; how the course of the design changes; all this occurs as a result of letting go of specific intent and permitting the design to evolve individually. Once I began to give myself this freedom I found that some of my previous imagery was combining with the blocks to form a new concept. An example is the inclusion of the fluid lines I had used in the concept drawing on page 64, and in the cabinet windows on page 58. The aggregate of these diverse styles can be seen in the library windows found on page 38-41.

This was the first drawing in the "Tumbling Block" series. The completed window is above left.

This drawing was one of the options proposed for the entry installation shown on page 65. The overall dimension of that entryway is 10' x 32' (3.1 x 9.9 m). Even though this design was never carried to fruition it was none the less an extraordinary experience to test the physical limits of this design style.

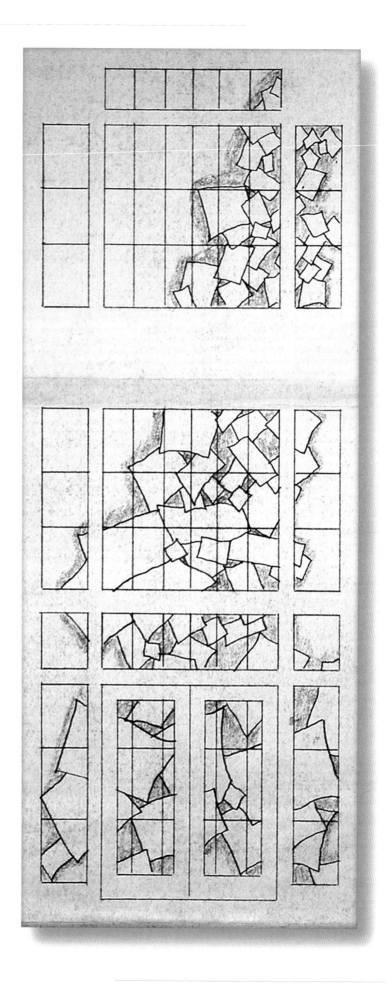

Title: "The Truth About Lying"

Title: " The First Tumble" - exterior view

Title: "Just A Taste"

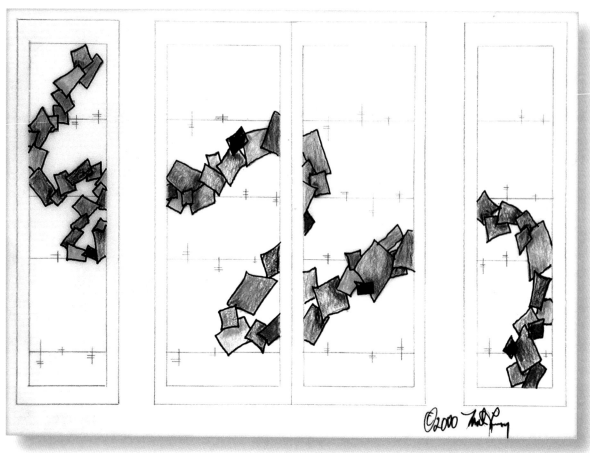

© 2000

© 2000

Title: "Mr. Robinson's Migraine"

The first window commission I completed for this client is shown at the top of page 25. After completing two additional projects, they asked me to submit a design for a fourth commission for their new kitchen window. As we informally discussed some design possibilities, Mr Robinson mentioned that he was prone to getting migraine headaches. He went on to describe them rather vividly as "sharp lightning bolts of color". I can't really say if it was his deliberate intention to propose his migraine description as an inspiration for my design but it struck me as an interesting challenge to interpret his vivid description in glass. To be sure, it was a most unusual subject to immortalize in glass. When I presented the colored renderings to them, he and his wife said I had captured the mental picture of his headaches perfectly. I used mouth blown full antique glass plus fracture & streamer glass to compose the color fields, while 3/4" thick beveled glass is used for the lightning bolts.

Title: "The First Tumble" - Detail (see page 33)

Title: "Come Together"

Windows from a Different Perspective

Title: "We Have A Winner"

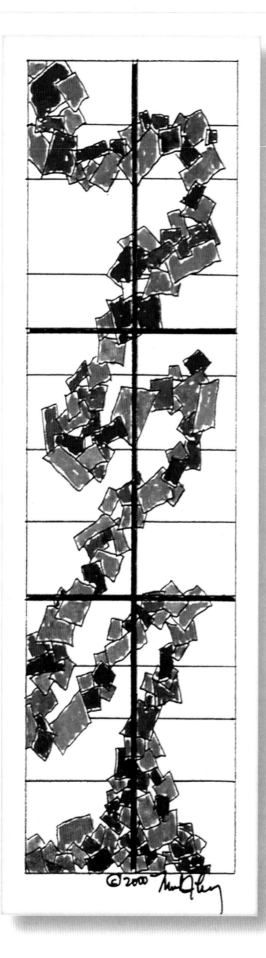

When I first discovered that the City of Los Angeles was building a new modern library in my area, I knew I wanted to be part of the project. A prominent public building offers the type of commission exposure that can have a profound benefit for any glass studio. While my previous experience with public commissions was limited, I was determined to write a successful proposal for the new library that the City would accept. I knew it was of the utmost importance to convey my vision to the Board of Library Commissioners, who were the granting agency. Of course I would demonstrate my experience and exhibit the depth of my previous works, but I needed to clearly explain how my work would enhance this public space. My goal from the outset was to create a powerful window design combined with a persuasive presentation in an all out effort to make it very difficult for the city to say no to my submission.

I was very gratified when my concept proposal was accepted. I worked closely with the city architect on specific issues of lighting, window frame and mullion positioning, and installation. The next step was for the glazing contractor to install the frame. Once installed I could take the detailed measurements of the negative and positive areas that were crucial to achieving the flowing visual movement I wanted in this design.

The overall height of the mural is 25' (7.75 m) which meant I had to set up a wall at my studio the same height to enable me to draw the full size pattern vertically and work on it as it would eventually be viewed.

The project architect requested that the color palette for the window was to be derived from the tones he specified in the carpeting. The actual selection of the texture, style and variety of glass was left to my discretion.

We completed the project and the installation went without a hitch. One of my special pleasures after any installation is to be the first eyewitness, to stand back and take in the sum and substance of a commission. I took particular delight that day knowing that the eye cannot absorb the entire visual intrigue at all times.

Title: "From Where I Have Come To I Don't Know Where" - Above & Right Installation Series

The author, Mark Levy, accepting a special commendation for his library window from Richard Riordan, the Mayor of Los Angeles

Once the mural had been installed, the responses were all very positive. The project architect commented that the window looked like it was always intended to have been included. This was very rewarding to hear, since the architect actually had to alter his original design plan to accommodate my window. The members of the Library Commission were all very delighted, as were the City Librarian and the Mayor. I was asked to attend the official grand opening of the new library. I had no idea, or even an inkling, that I was scheduled to receive a special commendation from the city. During the ceremony I was presented a beautiful commemorative proclamation, which I now have framed and hanging on my office wall.

Library window - Detail

Library window - Detail

Title: -"From Where I Have Come To I Don't Know Where"

Linear Organics

My architectural background has proven to be one of the strongest influences on my work. The basis for many of the pieces in this Linear Organics series is an abstraction of my architectural concepts regarding scale and proportion. The elements of architecture and the elements of visual artistic design are very similar and recognizing this relationship is key to creating a work that is sensitive to its environment. A good example of this is the room divider shown on page 46. The guiding factor in the design of this large expanse of glass was how to make it function in the house as an extension of the architecture. This consideration is important in all my work, but is particularly significant in these Linear Organic designs.

Another crucial element is the visual relationship between the type of glasswork and its setting within the living space. There will always be designs that are pure and independent. However I always endeavor to be aware of the rhythmic interaction of my work and the functional considerations of the installation. Should the work be bold and dramatic to become the focal point of the room, or should it be something more subtle to permit the focus to be on the room's primary function, the furniture and layout, or perhaps the people using the room. The organic quality that I strive for is to seamlessly mesh my work and the architectural space it occupies to create an indivisible single design element.

Title: "Opus #27"

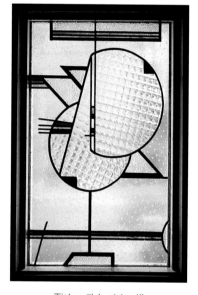

Title: "Untitled"

Title: "As The Path Narrows" - Interior Detail, See page 65 for exterior view of this installation.

© 2000

Title: -"Where The Path Can Go"

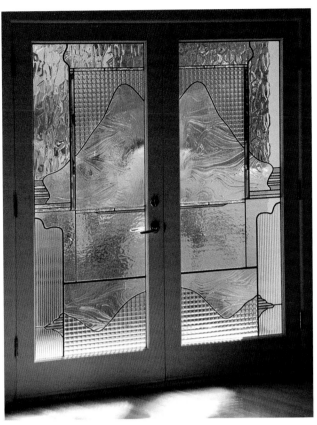

Title: -"Untitled"

Title: "Clearly Out Numbered"

Title: "Follow The Black"

The architect on this project requested a room divider 42' (13 m) in length that would separate the entrance gallery from the living area, but allow light to pass through. The conspicuous expanse of this divider required a resolute correlation between the existing architecture and the new mural. I decided to pick up two black bands of granite built into the adjoining fireplace wall (see detail photo at right), and carry this graphic element throughout my design. This unifies the entire expanse of glass, and is referenced in the title of "Follow The Black". I elected to use English Flemish glass for the entire expanse, which I cut in a variety of directions to focus the viewers eye on the graphic quality of the lines, rather than use a more complex palette of textured clears.

Title: "Follow The Black" Detail with fireplace

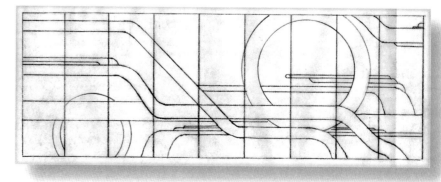

Title: "Three From Column A"

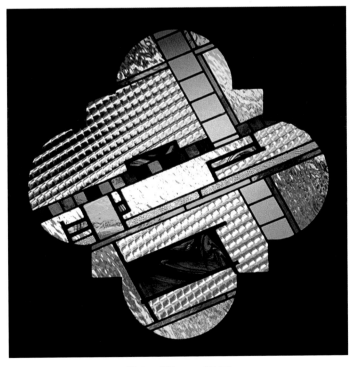

Title: "Opus #69"

The triptych above is in the home of an art gallery owner. She wanted a bold artistic statement but also wanted to obscure the view beyond her dining room window. I decided to layer the abstract images inside a matrix of columns to give the design depth and create an almost three dimensional illusion.

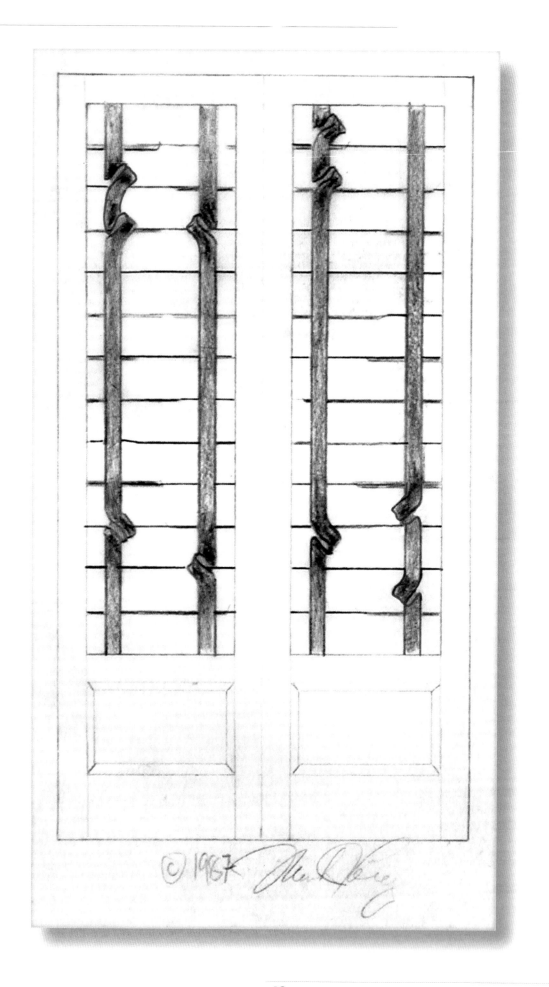

© 1987

Title: "Untitled"

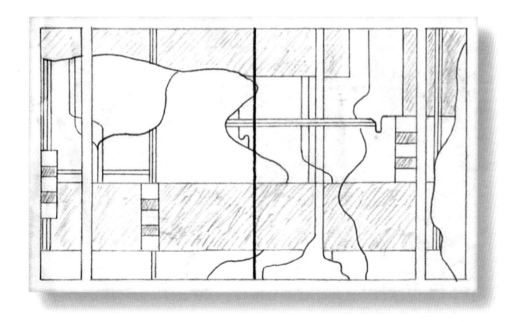

This drawing was proposed as a companion piece to the entry doors above. Unfortunately the construction budget got out of hand and the extra window space was eliminated from the adjoining room. It is disappointing when this happens, but eventually you get used to these kinds of things occurring.

Title: "You Shoulda' Seen The Look On Their Faces"

Title: "Atlantis Encounter"

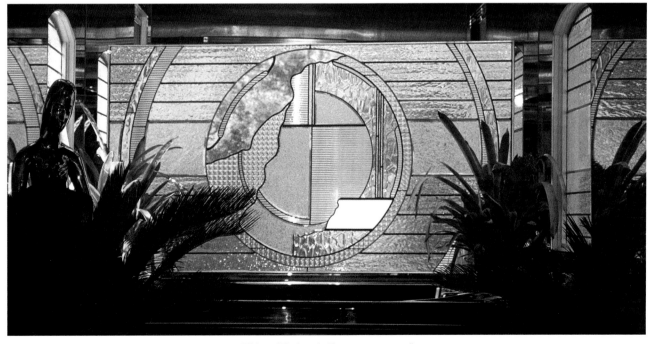

Title: "Esther's Extravaganza"

The architect on this project requested that I design the door, sidelight, the glass openings and the art glass. I created 4 different concepts, of which 3 are shown below. My clients final selection is shown in this photograph.

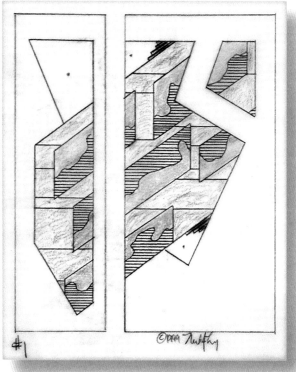

#1

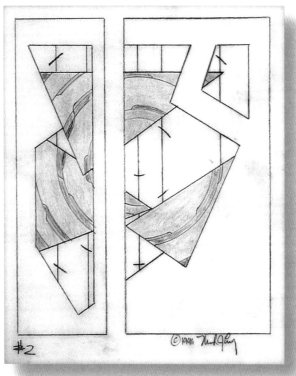

#2

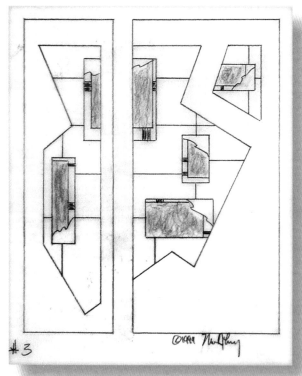

#3

T his proposal drawing was created for a client in Santa Barbara, California whose home was
located directly on the ocean. I was asked by the client to "create a design inspired by
water with the feeling of fluid motion".

Title: "Common Sense Isn't"

These editions of fireplace screens I designed were engineered to withstand the heat from a roaring fire, as well as function as artworks in and of themselves. There were 12 works in the series, and the one shown above is in the home of a well known art collector.

The drawing at right was designed for a working fireplace on a clients yacht; go figure!

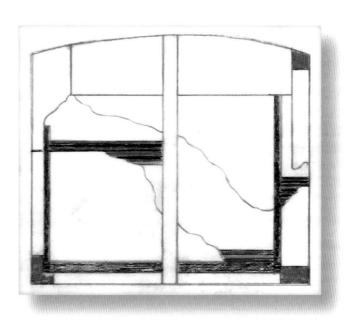

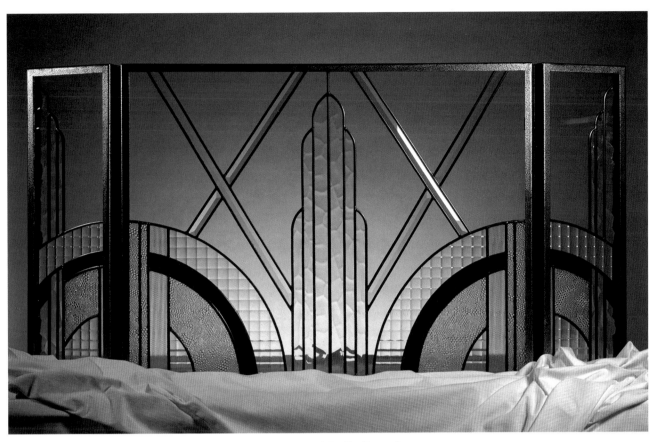

Title: "Decidedly Deco"

Title: "High Rise Heat"

For quite some time I had been pondering the general perception that leaded glass had to be contained in a geometrical form of some kind for example, a circle, a square, a rectangle, etc. I decided to experiment with works that used an irregular perimeter to define the shapes, with the proviso that the irregularity be part of the design itself. By permitting some of the design elements to expand beyond the traditional border of a contained form I could impart some attributes of kinetic energy. It was important to address the necessary engineering, and to maintain rigidity and strength. Once this was solved there was little restriction to the configuration or direction of the designs. In total I completed 8 screens in this series. As the series progressed each work became increasingly pronounced in its divergence from being limited to a standard geometrical perimeter shape.

Title: "The Only Push Ups I Know About Are The Ice Cream Kind"

The screen above right is steel framed and the glass inserts sit within this frame. This piece was acquired by an art collector and ended up being used in a television program!

The piece at left is installed in a high-gloss black lacquer "Coromondel" screen that can be folded both ways and adjusted to many configurations. I used a highly reflective black opal glass to mimic the shiny black finish on the wood. I wanted the viewer to be mystified by where one material ended, and the other began.

Title: "Mrs. Cora Mondales' Coromondel"

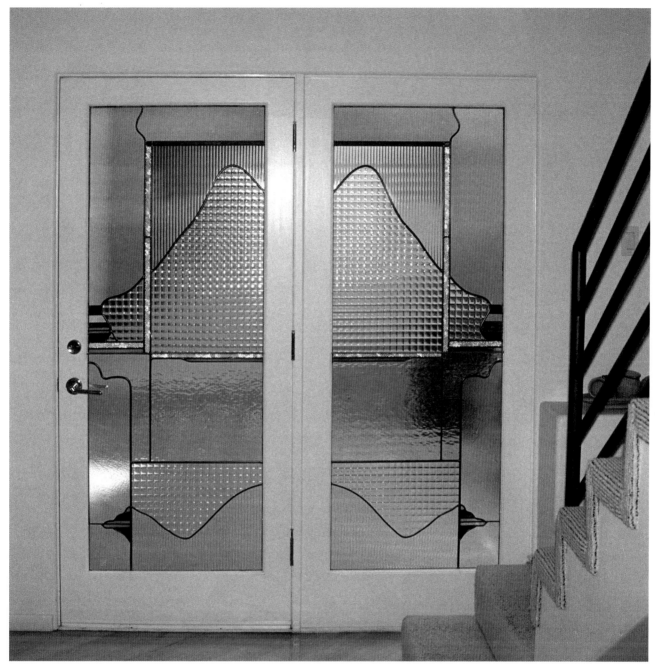

Title: "Engagement"

These doors are in one of 8 condominiums that make up a small, modern building in Santa Monica, California. The contractor told me that he wanted each unit to have something unique, but that he was working on a very tight budget. I was successful in designing a different concept for each unit and by using mostly domestic textured clear glass with small areas of imported antique.

I also managed to come in at the contractor's budget and all of his buyers were pleased with the installations.

It is possible to do good design on a very limited budget but it is important to keep the materials and fabrication requirements in mind at all times.

Title: "Follow The Bouncing Bevel"

My goal on this project was to create as much movement as possible within the design. The glass openings are small and the lead lines were strategically designed to move the eye of the viewer around and across the doors.

Title: "Follow The Bouncing Bevel"– 3 Cabinets & Wine Rack Detail

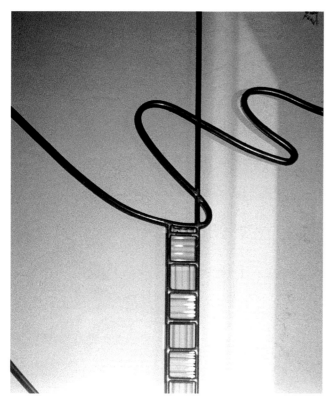

Title: "Follow The Bouncing Bevel"
Lead Detail

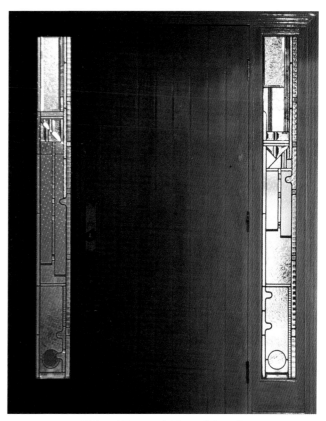

Title: "Ground Floor View"

This client (entry door, above right) wanted some privacy at their front door sidelights but they also have three small dogs that love to watch the world go by. In an effort to keep "everyone" happy I incorporated two small circles into my design placed at the dog's eye level and used standard clear window glass in them so the dogs could still have their "portholes" to the world.

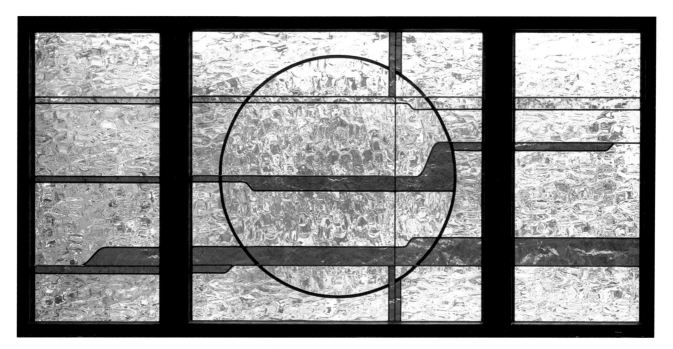

Title: "The Doctor Will See U Now"

Title: "Opus XVI"

Title: "China At Your Back Door"

After these panels (right) were completed, the project architect delivered them to his contractor for installation. The title "You've Got Me Upside Down And Backwards" refers to the fact that they were installed incorrectly, despite being clearly labeled for proper positioning. When I pointed this out to the architect he told me I should consider it to be a tribute to my work that the design worked even when installed improperly. Truth is he did not notice the error at installation and he preferred to not let his client know. However, a bit later when the client did eventually find out, we all had a good laugh.

Title: "You've Got Me Upside Down And Backwards"

Title: "Leave It To Leon"

Title: "Gilding The Lilies"

The designer on this commission asked for intensely dramatic windows that were going to be seen primarily in the evening. I tried to fool the eye into thinking that the ovals are the actual shape of the openings by designing "floating" interlocking ovals of color in a rectangular background of black opal glass. In the evening it does appear that way. I selected Fremont flashed full antique glass for its wonderful color gradations. (this glass also just happens to cut like a warm knife slicing through butter!!)

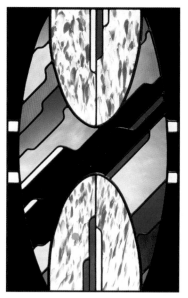

Title: "Gilding The Lilies" Detail

Title: "Just Suppose We Juxtapose"

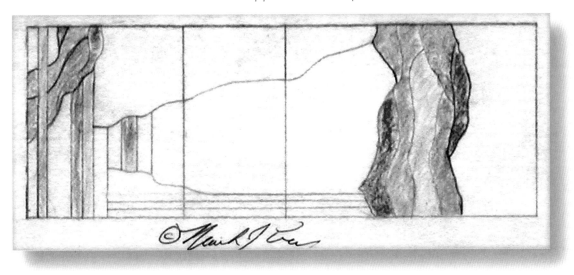

Title: "The Beginning Revisited"

Title: "Tien-An-Men Square On The Mend"

I was contacted by Winterthur Museum in Delaware regarding a home one of their benefactors was building on the Atlantic Ocean. The front entryway is 10' x 32' (3.1 x 9.9 m) and is composed of 14 individual panel sections. I was asked to do 5 different concepts for the space, based on previous works of mine they had seen on my website. The drawing at right is one of the concepts I submitted (see page 32 for one other example). The entrance photograph on the next page (page 65) is the design that was selected for fabrication. The completed entryway, although grand in scale, uses only two textures of clear glass, beveled optical lenses, and a small amount of colored European antique glass. (see page 43 for a detail photograph of the lower section of this entryway).

As an aside, it is always a good idea to show new clients previous artwork, as well as installation photos you have done for other projects. This proposal drawing was not selected to be used in the specific project for which it was designed, but by showing it to new prospective clients I was awarded two additional commissions. Consequently, any time invested in drawing and artwork is very worthwhile. You never know when a "pass" from one client may turn out to be just what another client was looking for.

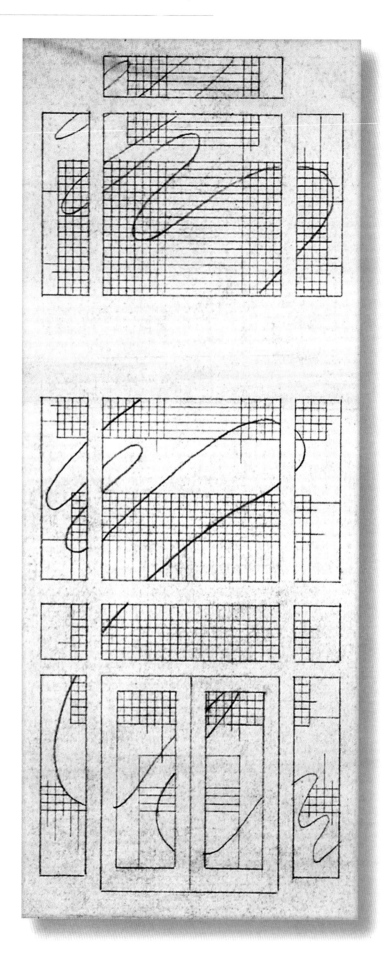

Title: "As The Path Narrows "

Title: "Mauve Moods"

Title: "Right Now, I'm Managing?"

A client, who was interested in one of my fireplace screens, contacted me for an appointment at my studio. During his visit he noticed some watercolor designs I was working on for a series of art panels. He was enamored by one design in particular that was for a window, but he had already finished his new home in Santa Fe, New Mexico and did not have a place for a window panel. What he did next is still remarkable to me. He instructed his contractor to re-engineer the newly completed home to create an opening in the exterior wall of his master bathroom for a stained glass window. Since this panel was part of an art series the client gave me free authority to choose the glass and colors. It is unlikely that I will ever encounter another client who will go to these great lengths in an effort to accommodate one of my works.

The window below is one of the first designs I completed in this series.

Title: "Stayin' Afloat"

Designers Divergence

Title: "Roman Rowen"

It is every artist's dream to have a client see their work, admire their design style and sensibilities, and then engage them for a wide-open commission. However, the artist is not always granted complete autonomy and from time to time may be asked to execute a design that differs from their own creative pursuit.

I feel it is important for me to be open to new design ideas. I am often gratified by the creative challenges presented by a commission that imposes design parameters that do not always coincide with my own. Each and every project I do refines and enhances my visual and technical skills. This influences all of my work, and as a result is a benefit to both my clients and myself. These commissions also provide an additional opportunity to have my work seen by as many people as possible.

I constantly strive to please myself, as well as my client, in whatever I do. My desire to be a successful artist often requires that I wear two hats, one for creative intent and one for business. As such, the driving force in my selection of commission work is to maintain a balance of the two. The freedom to work with a diverse blend of clients in a broad range of commissions is one I value tremendously. The potential to soar artistically, as well as professionally, can be found in each and every project.

Title: "Roman Rowen" detail

Title: "Untitled"

I allowed myself a great luxury while fabricating these windows. I was able to acquire 5 full sheets of European mouth blown antique (some of the most expensive art glass available), then choose the most perfect areas from each sheet that best suited the individual flowers. I carefully positioned each petal on the glass to take maximum advantage of the subtle shading in an effort to achieve the illusion of three-dimensional depth. (see detail on next page, lower left)

Title: "Judy's Glass Garland"

Title: "Acid Diamonds"

Title: "Untitled" - Detail (see page 70)

This client's home ("Acid Diamonds" window above) is decorated in a country English style with a flicker of Hobbit influences (ref: J.R.R. Tolkien's classic book "The Hobbit"). Rather than doing the traditional straight line diamond panel that might be expected in this kitchen bay window, I instead created these "Acid Diamonds". The idea was to interpret how ordinary leaded diamonds may have taken an altered shape within the context of J.R.R. Tolkien's "The Hobbit".

Title: "Untitled"

This one-of-a-kind beveled entryway features over 14,000" (5500 cm) of custom hand beveling. It includes doors, sidelites and five additional panels above, rising 30' (9.3 m) total. (Architect: Anne Hood)

Title: "What's Yours Is Yours"

Title: "Beyond Belief" – Full view

Title: "Beyond Belief" – Within Room Setting

udley Moore was, without hesitation, one of my all time favorite clients. I was given the privilege to design several windows in his home, and I asked him about this space in the kitchen. He replied that he simply wanted a row of flowerpots containing Poppies, with a shade to pull down for privacy in the evening, but no stained glass. I had an idea that I could do in glass what he wanted in reality. It was too good an opportunity to pass up. I set to work creating this design (at right), and when I presented it to him he immediately sat down at his piano and composed a quick little 'thank you' song for me right on the spot! I have learned that this window has since become his most favorite of all the installations.

Title: "Dudley's Delight"

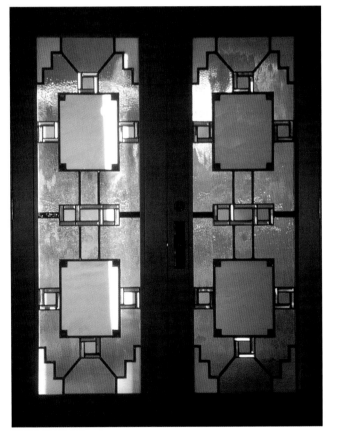

Title: "Fragile Fabric"

Title: "Untitled"

Two separate clients in Sedona, Arizona (where I had a studio) commissioned the sets of doors at left and above (cont. next page)

Title: "Moms' Reminder"

Title: "We'll Leave It Up To You"

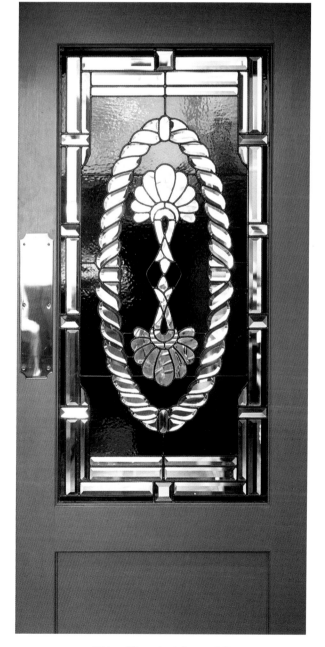

Title: "Beveled Squash"

(continued from page 74)
The designs at left are representations of actual rug patterns taken from Southwest Native American tribes. The glass was carefully selected for authentic color matches but the textural quality was just as important. I wanted to convey the feel of the glass to make it, as much as possible, like the original blankets themselves.

Title: "Well Urned Freedom" Room View

Title: "Untitled"

The entrance to this client's family room is through these four doors (above and right). The client wanted urns full of flowers as the motif, and I had to resolve the issue of how to design for the entire full height of the doors. I came up with the idea to place the urns on top of pedestals. I used several textures of clear glass and bevels to give the pedestals the life-like appearance of carved stone columns.

Windows from a Different Perspective

Title: "Well Urned Freedom" Detail View

Title: "Playing With The Planets" – Within Room Setting

These clients are devoted art glass collectors, and over the years have commissioned me to do more than 25 windows for them. Leonard is an inventor and a serious astronomer who actually has an observatory tower in his home that houses a rather large telescope. He gave me a tour of his observatory and when he touched a single button the observatory roof began to slowly open to expose the sky above, then the telescope extended up from its parked position until it was at eye level. He focused his telescope on the planets to give me a first hand look at the subject matter for these four panels. It was a real treat to actually see the planets in the sky and then use this experience as inspiration to see them later in the glass. I searched my glass rack for just the right glass pieces to accurately reproduce the color and texture of the planets, then I used copper foil overlay, glass paint, and sandblasting techniques to achieve the effect my client was after.

"Playing With The Planets – Earth"

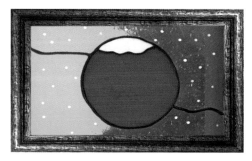

"Playing With The Planets – Mars"

"Playing With The Planets – Jupiter"

Title: "Playing With The Planets – Saturn"

INTRODUCTION TO ST GL
70 Pages - 17 Patterns

INITIATION AU VITRAIL
70 Pages - 17 Patterns

INITRODUCCIÓN AL VITRAL
70 Pages - 17 Patterns

QUICK SUCCESS ST GL
48 Pages - 18 Patterns

BEVEL WIN DESIGNS
100 Window Designs

CLASSIC ALPHABETS
48 Pages - 8 Patterns

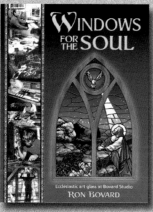

WIN's FOR THE SOUL
350 Color Photos

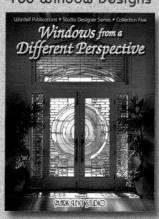

A DIFFERENT PERSPECTIVE
110 Color Photos

WINDOWS OF VISION
81 Color Photos

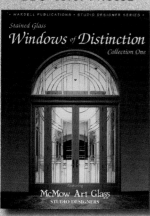

WIN's OF DISTINCTION
110 Color Photos

WIN's OF ELEGANCE
108 Color Photos

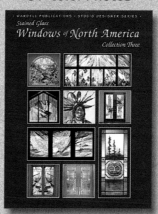

WIN's OF N. AMERICA
96 Color Photos

INSTRUCTION & RESOURCE BOOKS

Introduction to St. Gl. is available in English, Spanish & French. These do-it-yourself manuals presented in a step-by-step format covering all glass tools, supplies and techniques. Plus 17 full size project patterns designed for beginners. Quick Success St. Gl. is a course companion book. Classic Alphabets offers three complete lettering styles and two numeral styles for art glass signs & banner projects. 9x9 Lives is a project book featuring extensive instruction and templates for boxes, vases, trays, etc.

STAINED GLASS WINDOW BOOKS

This series books feature photographs and line drawings of spectacular stained glass window designs. The books in the "Studio Designer Series" contain inspiring collections of designer glass installations. The Windows for the Soul has 160 all color pages featuring sacred designs These books will be a valued addition to all art glass libraries and are essential for architects, interior designers, glass artists and everyone who appreciates beautiful glass.

Wardell
PUBLICATIONS INC
www.wardellpublications.com

FULL-SIZE PATTERNS FOR LAMPSHADES

This series of full-size pattern books contain over 110 lampshade designs ranging from small night-stand styles, to elaborate dining room show pieces.You will also find wall sconces, inverted ceiling style shades,.pool table lamps, and of course numerous shades suitable for either swag or lampbase applications. Each book contains comprehensive step-by-step instructions. All projects are shown in full color.

FULL-SIZE PATTERNS FOR DECORATIVE PROJECTS

These six books contain over 185 full-size patterns covering a wide range of project designs. Each book features a different subject theme including, terrariums, suncatchers, jewelry boxes, 3-D clocks, decorative mirrors, and much more. Step-by-step assembly instructions specific to the patterns contain fabrication tips and other helpful hints. All projects are shown photographed in color.

Wardell
PUBLICATIONS INC
www.wardellpublications.com

DESIGNS FOR LAMPS 1
18 Patterns

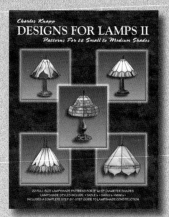

DESIGNS FOR LAMPS II
22 Patterns

LAMPWORKS
16 Patterns

LAMPSHADE PATTERNS I
22 Patterns

LAMPSHADE PATTERNS II
11 Patterns

NORTHERN SHADES
25 Patterns

CLOCK GALLERY
18 Patterns

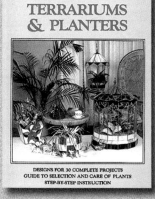

TERRARIUMS & PLANTERS
30 Patterns

WALL DECORATIONS
29 Patterns

STAINED GLASS BOXES
34 Patterns

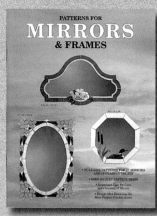

MIRRORS & FRAMES
43 Patterns

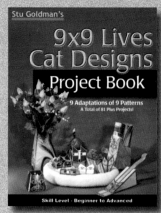

9x9 LIVES CAT DESIGNS
48 Pages - 9X9 Patterns